FLUTE

RODGERS AND HAMMERSTEIN™

Contents

WILLIAMSON MUSIC®

A RODGERS AND HAMMERSTEIN COMPANY

EXCLUSIVELY DISTRIBUTED BY

HAL•LEONARD®
CORPORATION

7777 W. BLUEMOUND RD. P.O. BOX 13819 MILWAUKEE, WI 53213

Cover Designed by FRANK "FRAVER" VERLIZZO

THE SOUND OF MUSIC
(From "THE SOUND OF MUSIC")

Lyrics by OSCAR HAMMERSTEIN II
Music by RICHARD RODGERS

Flute

CLIMB EV'RY MOUNTAIN
(From "THE SOUND OF MUSIC")

Lyrics by OSCAR HAMMERSTEIN II
Music by RICHARD RODGERS

Flute

DO-RE-MI
(From "THE SOUND OF MUSIC")

Lyrics by OSCAR HAMMERSTEIN II
Music by RICHARD RODGERS

EDELWEISS
(From "THE SOUND OF MUSIC")

Lyrics by OSCAR HAMMERSTEIN II
Music by RICHARD RODGERS

Flute

Slowly, with expression

I HAVE CONFIDENCE
(From "THE SOUND OF MUSIC")

Lyrics and Music by
RICHARD RODGERS

Flute

THE LONELY GOATHERD

(From "THE SOUND OF MUSIC")

Lyrics by OSCAR HAMMERSTEIN II
Music by RICHARD RODGERS

Flute

MARIA
(From "THE SOUND OF MUSIC")

Lyrics by OSCAR HAMMERSTEIN II
Music by RICHARD RODGERS

Flute

Allegretto con moto

Moderately

11

MY FAVORITE THINGS
(From "THE SOUND OF MUSIC")

Lyrics by OSCAR HAMMERSTEIN II
Music by RICHARD RODGERS

Flute

SO LONG, FAREWELL
(From "THE SOUND OF MUSIC")

Lyrics by OSCAR HAMMERSTEIN II
Music by RICHARD RODGERS

Flute

SIXTEEN GOING ON SEVENTEEN
(From "THE SOUND OF MUSIC")

Lyrics by OSCAR HAMMERSTEIN II
Music by RICHARD RODGERS

Flute

SOMETHING GOOD
(From "THE SOUND OF MUSIC")

Lyrics and Music by
RICHARD RODGERS

Flute